The
the Bird,
the Beetle,
and Me

Written by Sarah Prince

Illustrated by Ulrich Lehman

 sundance

If I were a butterfly
fluttering by,
what would I see
with my little eyes?

If I flew across the grass,
it would look like
a huge green carpet.

Everything would look
big, and the flowers would
be bigger than me.

The leaves would
look like giant
umbrellas.
I could hide
underneath them.

If I were a bird
flying so high,
what would I see
from up in the sky?

If I looked down from
way up high,
I could see the houses
and the gardens.

It would look like
a giant quilt with lots of
different colors.

I could fly up high
and see the mountains
or fly back down and
visit the sea.

If I were a beetle
so black and shiny,
what would I see
if I were so tiny?

I could crawl to the top
of a pumpkin.
It would be like a
mountain to me.

But I couldn't
stay up there —
I'd have to hide
so I wouldn't get eaten!

I could live my life
on the ground
and have adventures every day.

But I'm not a beetle
or a bird in a tree.
I'm not a butterfly.
Here's what I see.

What do you see?